CW00410872

George Catlin (1796–1872). *Breaking Down the Wild Horse*, ca. 1837. Oil on canvas, 25³/₁₆ × 31½ in. The Rockwell Museum, bequest of Clara S. Peck.

William M. Cary (1840–1922). *Indians Jousting*, 1875. Oil on canvas, 5¹¹/₁₆ × 10⅝ in. The Rockwell Company.

Frank Tenney Johnson (1874–1939). *Branding*, date unknown. Oil on canvas, 36⅜ × 46³/₁₆ in. The Rockwell Museum, gift of Thomas K. Figgee.

Charles M. Russell (1864–1926). *A Mix Up*, 1910. Oil on canvas, 30 × 48 in. The Rockwell Museum.

1 (outside) William M. Cary, *Indians Jousting*, 1875

2 (inside) Charles M. Russell, *A Mix Up*, 1910

Carl Rungius (1861–1959). *The Monarchs of the Wilderness,* ca. 1901. Oil on canvas, 36 × 55 in. The Rockwell Museum.

William M. Cary (1840–1922). *The Upper Missouri,* 1875. Oil on canvas, 14⅝ × 27⅜ in. The Rockwell Company.

Walter Ufer (1876–1936). *Along the Rio Grande,* 1920. Oil on canvas, 24½ × 24½ in. The Rockwell Museum.

Thomas Moran (1837–1927). *Clouds in the Canyon,* 1915. Oil on canvas, 19⅝ × 24⅜ in. The Rockwell Museum.

9 (*outside*) Harvey Dunn. *Montana Winter Scene*, 1907.

11 (*outside*) John Mix Stanley. *The Smoke Signal*, 1868.

14 (*outside*) Frederic Remington. *The Arizona Cowboy*, 1901.

16 (*outside*) Charles M. Russell. *Cowboy*, 1904.

Henry Farny (1847–1916). *The Sign of Peace*, 1508. Oil on panel, 39¾ × 21¾ in. The Rockwell Museum, bequest of Clara S. Peck.

Frederic Remington (1861–1909). *The Arizona Cowboy*, 1901. Pastel on paper, 29¾ × 23½ in. The Rockwell Museum.

Charles M. Russell (1864–1926). *The Piegan Chief*, 1912. Watercolor on paper, 14 × 12 in. Robert F. Rockwell, Jr.

Charles M. Russell (1864–1926). *Cowboy*, 1904. Watercolor on paper, 15½ × 11½ in. Hertha Rockwell.

Charles Schreyvogel (1861–1912). *Dead Sure*, 1902. Oil on canvas, 19¾ × 15¾ in. The Rockwell Museum.

William H. Dunton (1878–1936). *Bronco Buster*, ca. 1905. Oil on canvas, 39 × 25 in. The Rockwell Museum, gift of William C. Whitridge.

Paul Frenzeny (ca. 1840–1902). *Indian Scouting Party*, ca. 1875. Watercolor on paper, 17¾ × 10¾ in. The Rockwell Museum, bequest of Clara S. Peck.

Charles Schreyvogel (1861–1912). *An Unexpected Enemy*, 1900. Oil on canvas, 33¾ × 24¾ in. The Rockwell Museum.

17 (outside) Charles Schreyvogel, *Dead Sure*, 1902

Charles M. Russell (1864–1926). *Stolen Horses*, 1898. Oil on academy board, 17¾ × 23⅝ in. The Rockwell Museum.

William R. Leigh (1866–1955). *The Great Buffalo Hunt,* 1947. Oil on canvas, 78⅜ × 127⅜ in. The Rockwell Museum.

William H. Dunton (1878–1936). *The Helping Hand,* 1910. Oil on canvas, 24½ × 37½ in. The Rockwell Company.

Alfred Jacob Miller (1810–1874). *Crow Indian on Horseback,* 1844. Oil on canvas, 19⁹⁄₁₆ × 25⅜ in. The Rockwell Museum, bequest of Clara S. Peck.